D1622143

PRO WRESTLING'S GREATEST
HEELS

BY MATT SCHEFF

SportsZone

An Imprint of Abdo Publishing
abdopublishing.com

abdopublishing.com

Published by Abdo Publishing, a division of ABDO, PO Box 398166, Minneapolis, Minnesota 55439. Copyright © 2017 by Abdo Consulting Group, Inc. International copyrights reserved in all countries. No part of this book may be reproduced in any form without written permission from the publisher. SportsZone™ is a trademark and logo of Abdo Publishing.

Printed in the United States of America, North Mankato, Minnesota
092016
012017

Cover Photo: Mel Evans/AP Images
Interior Photos: Mel Evans/AP Images, 1; CD1 WENN Photos/Newscom, 4; Matt Roberts/ZumaPress/Newscom, 5; Sharkpixs/ZumaPress/Newscom, 6–7; Rick Scuteri/WWE/AP Images, 8–9; Domine Jerome/Sipa USA/AP Images, 10–11; Victoria Arocho/AP Images, 12–13; Bill Olive/Getty Images, 14–15; John Barrett/ZumaPress/Newscom, 16–17; Snapper Media/Splash News/Newscom, 18–19; Nasser Berzane/ZumaPress/Newscom, 20–21; Marc Serota/AP Images for Wrestlemania, 22–23; George Pimentel/Getty Images, 24–25; Paul Fenton/ZumaPress/Newscom, 26; Smock John/SIPA/Newscom, 27; Carlos Osorio/AP Images, 28; Tom Strattman/AP Images, 29

Editor: Patrick Donnelly
Series Designer: Laura Polzin

Publisher's Cataloging-in-Publication Data
Names: Scheff, Matt, author.
Title: Pro wrestling's greatest heels / by Matt Scheff.
Description: Minneapolis, MN : Abdo Publishing, 2017. | Series: Pro wrestling's
    greatest | Includes bibliographical references and index.
Identifiers: LCCN 2016945634 | ISBN 9781680784954 (lib. bdg.) |
    ISBN 9781680798234 (ebook)
Subjects: LCSH: Wrestling--Juvenile literature.
Classification: DDC 796.812--dc23
LC record available at http://lccn.loc.gov/2016945634

TABLE OF CONTENTS

INTRODUCTION: NO MORE MR. NICE GUY

Few tag teams in wrestling history have been more popular than the Rockers. Partners Shawn Michaels and Marty Jannetty worked their way up the pro wrestling ranks together. When they finally made it to World Wrestling Entertainment (WWE), fans loved them. Nothing could match their high-flying, energetic style. But that all ended in 1991.

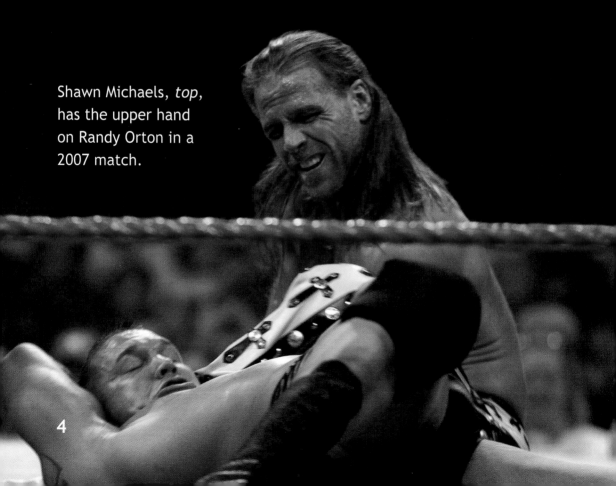

Shawn Michaels, *top*, has the upper hand on Randy Orton in a 2007 match.

Shawn Michaels
loved playing
the heel.

The partners appeared on the WWE talk show *The Barber Shop*. Michaels waited until Jannetty was distracted. Then he lashed out with a superkick. He sent Jannetty flying through a window. The friendship was over. Michaels had turned into a heel.

Michaels became one of the great heels in WWE history.

THE HEEL TURN

One of the biggest moments in pro wrestling is a heel turn. It's the moment where a babyface—or a good guy—turns into a heel. A heel turn usually comes when a babyface betrays a friend or a partner. And the bigger the babyface, the more shocking the heel turn.

TEN

"MILLION DOLLAR MAN" TED DiBIASE

Ted DiBiase was WWE's richest wrestler. He loved to shove his wealth in the faces of opponents and fans. When he'd pin an opponent, DiBiase would stuff a $100 bill into his opponent's mouth. Once, DiBiase offered a young fan $500 if he could dribble a basketball 15 times. On dribble number 14, DiBiase kicked the ball away.

Ted DiBiase, *center*, joined by sons Ted Jr., *left*, and Brett, is inducted into the WWE Hall of Fame in 2010.

NINE

KEVIN OWENS

It didn't take Kevin Owens long to become one of WWE's most hated heels. He introduced himself to fans in 2015 by stomping on John Cena's US Championship belt. That set up an instant feud with Cena, one of the most popular pro wrestlers in the world. Owens fueled the fire by mocking and teasing opponents. He's a classic bully, and fans love to boo him for it.

Kevin Owens angered fans when he challenged John Cena, one of WWE's most popular performers.

EIGHT

SHAWN MICHAELS

For years, Shawn Michaels was a babyface. He built a huge fan base as a member of The Rockers tag team. But that changed in 1991 when he made a heel turn. He attacked partner Marty Jannetty. Michaels called himself "the Heartbreak Kid." Fans who once loved him instantly booed him.

Shawn Michaels embraced the role of the heel once he turned his back on former partner Marty Jannetty.

Roddy Piper, *right*, was rowdy in the ring and not much better on the outside.

SEVEN

"ROWDY" RODDY PIPER

"Rowdy" Roddy Piper was one of the great villains of WWE in the 1980s. He was a rival to fan-favorite Hulk Hogan. Piper was a heel in the ring and out. He hosted his own talk show, *Piper's Pit*. There, he insulted fellow wrestlers. He once smashed a coconut over the head of babyface Jimmy "Superfly" Snuka.

RIVALRIES

Pro wrestling is famous for its bitter rivalries. Fans like watching the back-and-forth feuds between babyfaces and heels. The more rotten the heel, the more fans care about the rivalry.

SIX

BOBBY "THE BRAIN" HEENAN

Bobby "The Brain" Heenan wasn't really a wrestler at all. But he was still one of WWE's all-time heels. Heenan split his time as a manager for some of WWE's most hated heels and as an annoying ringside commentator. In the 1980s and 1990s, he was the voice of the heels in WWE.

Bobby "The Brain" Heenan temporarily set aside his heel role when he was inducted into the WWE Hall of Fame in 2004.

FIVE

RIC FLAIR

Ric Flair was often referred to as "the dirtiest player in the game." There was no trick he wouldn't use to cheat his way to victory. Flair spent 40 years as a pro wrestler. Over that time, he feuded with greats such as Ricky "The Dragon" Steamboat, Edge, and Hulk Hogan.

NICKNAMES

Nicknames are a big part of pro wrestling. Rocky Maivia became "The Rock." Ric Flair became "Nature Boy." And Steve Austin became "Stone Cold." Nicknames give wrestlers a little extra excitement and make them seem larger than life.

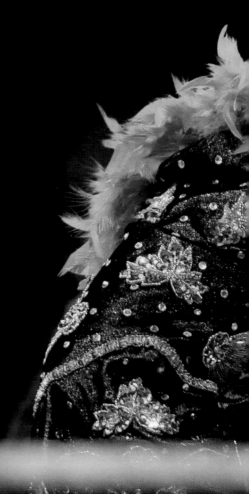

Few wrestlers took to the role of heel as naturally as Ric Flair.

FOUR

TRIPLE H

Triple H was an all-around bad guy. In the late 1990s and early 2000s, he feuded with babyfaces Steve Austin and The Rock. "The Cerebral Assassin" was cold-blooded inside the ring and out. He married Stephanie McMahon, the daughter of WWE boss Vince McMahon. Injuries curtailed his career. But he remains a key part of WWE, serving as its chief operating officer.

Triple H knew just how to intimidate opponents and amp up the crowd.

THREE

CM PUNK

Some heels seem bad to the core. Others just enjoy annoying fans. That's CM Punk. The self-named "Straight Edge Savior" loved to tell the fans how they should live their lives. And they loved to hate him for it. Punk made his name as the rival to fan-favorite John Cena. His mixed martial arts training allowed him to back up all his big talk with results in the ring.

CM Punk has Chris Jericho in trouble at WrestleMania 28 in 2012.

23

TWO

"HOLLYWOOD" HULK HOGAN

At first, Hulk Hogan was beloved by fans. He was one of the greatest babyfaces in wrestling history. "Hulkamania" helped launch WWE into the biggest pro wrestling promotion in the world. Hogan was in movies, video games, and TV advertisements. That's what made his heel turn such a shock. As the evil "Hollywood" Hulk Hogan, he cheated and bullied his way back to the top. Fans who had loved him suddenly hated him.

"Hollywood" Hulk Hogan cut an intimidating figure in the ring.

ONE

VINCE McMAHON

Vince McMahon did it all. He owned and operated WWE. He was a ringside commentator. And in the late 1990s, he became the greatest villain pro wrestling has ever seen. McMahon's feud with fan-favorite "Stone Cold" Steve Austin never seemed to end. And Austin always seemed to get the best of it.

Vince McMahon is one of the richest executives in the sports world.

Vince McMahon showed his heel side whenever a microphone was in front of him.

McMahon would do anything to build on his bad reputation. He bullied WWE stars into taking his side. He fired those who wouldn't. McMahon even had his own daughter kidnapped in a plot to steal the title from Austin. Anyone who stepped up to oppose McMahon earned instant favor with fans. He was the perfect heel and helped raise WWE to its highest levels of popularity.

McMahon gets his head shaved by Donald Trump, *left*, and wrestler Bobby Lashley in 2007.

McMahon played the heel role to help build the popularity of WWE.

GLOSSARY

BABYFACE
A wrestler seen as a good guy;
also called a face.

BETRAY
Be disloyal to an ally.

CEREBRAL
Intelligent or thoughtful.

COMMENTATOR
A television announcer for
a wrestling match or other
sporting event.

DISTRACTED
Not concentrating or
paying attention.

FEUD
A bitter disagreement between
two or more people.

HEEL
A wrestler seen as a villain.

HEEL TURN
The event that marks the
changing of a good guy
(babyface) into a villain (heel).

RIVALRY
A long-standing, intense, and
often emotional competition
between two people or teams.

TAG TEAM
Two or more wrestlers working
together to win a match against
a group of opponents.

FOR MORE INFORMATION

BOOKS

Kortemeier, Todd. *Superstars of WWE*. Mankato, MN: Amicus High Interest, 2016.

Scheff, Matt. *Pro Wrestling's Greatest Rivalries*. Minneapolis, MN: Abdo Publishing, 2017.

WEBSITES

To learn more about pro wrestling, visit booklinks.abdopublishing.com. These links are routinely monitored and updated to provide the most current information available.

INDEX

ABOUT THE AUTHOR

Matt Scheff is an artist and author living in Alaska. He enjoys mountain climbing, deep-sea fishing, and curling up with his two Siberian huskies to watch wrestling.